HOW TO GROW YOUR HOME CARE/ HOSPICE BUSINESS

5 Steps to Success in Growing your Agency

Cheryl Peltekis, RN "The Solutionist"

Copyright © 2014 Cheryl Peltekis, RN "The Solutionist".

All rights reserved. No part of this book may be used or reproduced by any means, graphic, electronic, or mechanical, including photocopying, recording, taping or by any information storage retrieval system without the written permission of the author except in the case of brief quotations embodied in critical articles and reviews.

Balboa Press books may be ordered through booksellers or by contacting:

Balboa Press
A Division of Hay House
1663 Liberty Drive
Bloomington, IN 47403
www.balboapress.com
844-682-1282

Because of the dynamic nature of the Internet, any web addresses or links contained in this book may have changed since publication and may no longer be valid. The views expressed in this work are solely those of the author and do not necessarily reflect the views of the publisher, and the publisher hereby disclaims any responsibility for them.

The author of this book does not dispense medical advice or prescribe the use of any technique as a form of treatment for physical, emotional, or medical problems without the advice of a physician, either directly or indirectly. The intent of the author is only to offer information of a general nature to help you in your quest for emotional and spiritual well-being. In the event you use any of the information in this book for yourself, which is your constitutional right, the author and the publisher assume no responsibility for your actions.

Any people depicted in stock imagery provided by Getty Images are models, and such images are being used for illustrative purposes only. Certain stock imagery © Getty Images.

Print information available on the last page.

ISBN: 979-8-7652-3732-8 (sc)
ISBN: 979-8-7652-3731-1 (hc)
ISBN: 979-8-7652-3730-4 (e)

Library of Congress Control Number: 2022922688

Balboa Press rev. date: 01/26/2023

Contents

Dedication vii
Introduction ix

1 Who Am I, and Why Should You Listen to Me? 1
2 A Moment of Fear 7
3 The Beginning of a Lean, Mean Sales Machine 11
4 Our Journey Begins 17
5 The First Step: Study 21
6 The Second Step: Accounts and Accountability 31
7 Step Three: Lead 41
8 Expectations and Excellence 51
9 Success 59
10 Maintain Success 63
11 Replication and Conclusion 69

Bibliography 73

Dedication

I would like to dedicate this book to my family. To my loving husband, business partner, and best friend, Bill, thank you for all your love and support! To my five wonderful children, Eleni, Nicolette, Thomas, Alexandra, and Angela, I love you all so much. I am so proud of the adults that you have become. To my incredible parents, Mark and Shirley Hawkins, and my in-laws, Eleni and Athanasios Peltekis, I love you all. And to my wonderful sister, Denise, I couldn't have done this without you. I would also like to thank all the great employees and patients who touched my heart over the years. Some of the best times in my life were in your company. Thank you!

Introduction

I never thought I would write a book. I always felt I was the worst writer ever to graduate from Cardinal Dougherty High School—but then something happened. I had something that I truly needed to share with other owners of homecare, hospice, and private duty companies. I realized that I had developed a process to grow any organization, and that I could replicate the process. I tried it at several agencies for free, and it worked. Once I was able to prove such success, I opened my own consulting company—Penta Care Consulting. The name is an acronym for my family: P–Peltekis, E–Eleni, N–Nicolette, T–Tommy, A–A-team, which is how we refer to Alexandra and Angela. The acronym is even in their birth order. Now I have joined Power Shot Training, and we're part of a team that can truly transform any organization.

What happened to motivate a mom of five, who owns two businesses, four homes, multiple rental properties, and has more than one hundred employees, to stop and write a book? I want to show you how to transform your organization and your life—to give you the lifestyle you long for, and make it come true for you. You deserve it. It is incredibly satisfying to be a value-producing human being in this world. Our organizations allow us to employ people in our communities which, in turn, allows others to have abundance in their lives. What a gift to others and to ourselves. Thank you God for all your blessing, joyful abundance, and health that everyone in this industry has been able to give.

I want to share my success and what motivated me to go get it.

1

Who Am I, and Why Should You Listen to Me?

I GREW UP IN A ROW HOME IN PHILADELPHIA. We referred to it as the Hawkins family nursing home. Neither of my parents had a college degree, but how to love was not something you had to learn in college. My parents gave my brother, sister, and me all the love and confidence we needed to be successful. We went to church every Sunday. I played guitar and sang at Mass every week.

Then a drunk driver killed my brother when he was sixteen. I was just nine years old at the time. Mark's death was extremely difficult for my family. God helped us all heal, and we were able to move on with all the fond memories in our hearts.

When I was thirteen, I started in health care as a volunteer at a local hospital within walking distance—Parkview Hospital. I worked in the physical therapy department. I helped transport patients from their hospital rooms to therapy. I also had the fun task of cleaning the whirlpool tubs. It was a great experience, and it introduced me to the ways a patient can rehabilitate after an acute event. I have been in health care now for more than thirty-three years.

As mentioned earlier, I grew up in the Hawkins family nursing home. My great-grandmother had Alzheimer's, and my mom would have her over several days of the week. I would come home from school, go upstairs to the linen closet, take out all the clean towels, unfold them, and place them in a laundry basket. I would take the laundry to my great-grandma and ask her if she would help me fold it. Of course, I knew that she wouldn't offer to help but, would say, "Oh, honey, you don't have to help me. I can do it for you." Keeping great-grandma busy freed my mom and allowed her to make dinner for our family.

My grandmother lived with us for a time, as did my grandfather and my great-aunt. She lived with us for fifteen years. I moved out when I was twenty-two, so I lived with her my entire life. We also had a cousin who lived with us for a while because she was having chemotherapy and radiation for breast cancer, and the cancer treatment hospital was too far from her home. I was born into being a caretaker. I am so lucky to have been raised in this environment, and I wouldn't have changed my experience for anyone else's. These life experiences gave me the tools to truly understand the customers I service today.

My mom died in 2006 after losing her nine-year battle with ovarian cancer. What's ironic is that my first nursing job when I was twenty-two was working at the first hospital in the nation, Pennsylvania Hospital, on a floor dedicated to GYN oncology, so I knew what death for a patient with ovarian cancer looked like. I remember having lost a young woman to ovarian cancer, with her young children at her bedside in the hospital. That night, I came home from work and told my husband what a terrible death she had.

When my mom was diagnosed with ovarian cancer, I was truly aware of what was to come. While my mom was on hospice/palliative care through a local company, she listened to me as I worked on my future hospice company's policies. She made many contributions to my hospice company's planning. We branded the company in the color teal, which is the color that represents ovarian cancer.

I have lost a brother, my mother, and all my grandparents, some of whom I was very close to because we lived in the same home. I had a twenty-four-week fetal demise with my fourth pregnancy. I know grief, and I know caregiving. I have run a home care and hospice organization since 1995. This organization has been deficiency free since its inception, and has received seven gold seals of approval by the Joint Commission on Accreditation.

But what does my life story have to do with being able to have a successful sales program? Well, how we react to stress or pressure is defined by our life experiences. I worked so hard to build a successful business that I was truly passionate about. When I saw it slipping away because of competition and realized my organization was making no effort to regain our market share, I was afraid.

I had been here once before. In July 1995, the first year we opened our company, it took forever for the first check to come from Medicare. I had a newborn, and my grandfather would come with me to work every day and stay with the baby. His presence allowed me to have her at work with me and feed her whenever she was hungry. Grandpa would do the burping, change the diapers, and navigate (no GPS back then). He was also my friend.

One day, my sister called me on my cell phone (a big box phone, back then) to tell me that we were not going to make payroll on Friday. We were $7,000 short. We had been running the business for twelve months without being paid a dollar.

We used every credit card we had to pay bills, and we had already borrowed from anyone who would lend us money. I had nothing left. I felt so terrible because I had failed. I hung up the phone, and my grandfather asked me what was wrong. I didn't tell him. I said she called because we had run out of stamps. When we got back to the office after my visits were done, my grandfather went to my sister and asked why she had called me. He told her that I seemed upset. Well, she told him.

The next day, I went to pick up my grandfather as usual, and when he got into my car, he asked if we could stop at his bank sometime before noon. We went there between visits; after my last visit, my grandfather asked me to stop at another bank. I said sure and asked where. He said, "Whatever bank has your payroll account." He had taken out $7,000 and was handing it to me. I was so thankful for his help. The next day I received the first check from Medicare, and we were saved—for the time being.

2

A Moment of Fear

I WAS AFRAID AGAIN FOURTEEN YEARS later—yes, pure, stare-in-your-face fear. It's truly astonishing what people will do when they fear for the lives of their children and are facing a significant downward spiral. Then you look at the faces of your fifty employees. These are incredible people, some of whom you have worked with for the last fourteen years. You know their families—whose birthday is coming up, who is saving to take their children to Disneyland for the first time, who is trying to help pay for a child's college tuition, a baptism, a wedding, a bar mitzvah, a first home, a first child, a first car. And you wonder how you will choose which ones to lay off.

Once I stopped feeling sorry for myself (which lasted about ten minutes), I knew I had to act fast. I had to risk it all once again as I had with my start-up fourteen years earlier. I also knew that my husband Bill would not want to risk it all again. He was more concerned because this time we had five children to support, and the risk was no longer one we took alone, as with our start-up. When we started our first business, it was just him, me, and two infants. If it failed, we would just have to go back and work full-time in the hospital. We would maybe lose our house, but so what? We would rebuild. Now, we had five other mouths to feed. We had tutors to pay, sports, dance, cheerleading, violin, piano lessons, and ice hockey. I had to convince Bill to let me take a big risk once again.

Many of you are probably saying, "She doesn't know my market and how much competition I have in my area." You're right, but I will tell you this: when my husband and I started the company in 1995, there were about nineteen providers in our five counties. By 2007, that number had grown to more than one hundred, and it was still on the rise. We had five times more competition than we did when my husband and I started. Our marketplace had also experienced a large shift in traditional Medicare. Seniors in Philadelphia went from 100 percent having traditional Medicare to 20 percent having Medicare and 80 percent having Medicare-managed care. As a result, we were losing not only market share but also revenue.

My first task was to convince my husband that we needed to take a risk, but he was afraid we wouldn't be able to provide for our family and didn't want to risk any more money. I also knew, though, that he loved me blindly. He would follow me anywhere I would lead him. He would be my rock. So when I shared with him that the company was losing more than $180,000 in 2009 (the third consecutive year in the red), I was afraid he would want to just walk away. I knew he would want to lay off everyone and have the two of us work twenty-four hours a day to avoid more losses. But I wanted to hire a sales representative to try to reclaim the marketplace. Bill said, "Are you kidding me? We can't pay our bills now, and you want to increase the budget?"

"Well," I said, "Isn't that what our line of credit and credit cards are for?" I wanted to save my company. I wanted to save my family's lifestyle. I wanted to save my employees' jobs. I wanted to continue to service the neediest clients in Philadelphia for as many years as I possibly could. Failure wasn't an option for me.

My husband once again took the leap of faith and told me he knew I would never be okay with failing at the business unless I exhausted all chances of saving it. He gave me a big kiss and said, "Go get them," and that's exactly what I did.

3

The Beginning of a Lean, Mean Sales Machine

NEXT I FOUND EVERYONE WHO WAS IN the homecare/hospice business development world—everyone who was teaching people sales and marketing. Some called themselves gurus or hotshots. I went to more than five different training sessions across this country from March to July 2009. Some lasted more than three days and were called Boot Camps, Sales Universities, and Power Sales Trainings. Each guru had different methods to suggest, but none of them had ever been in my predicament.

One of the largest consulting companies for home care and hospice had a salesman doing the training. He was eager, but he wasn't a nurse, wasn't a business owner, and didn't have a single employee to think about. He hadn't just poured every ounce of himself into creating a company. I felt that none of the experts out there understood me. The ones I found who could relate to operational issues were clueless about sales and marketing. When I returned home, I got to work. I spent the next ninety days (August through October) reading. I read stories from accomplished entrepreneurs, and I made a list of different philosophies or processes that I would follow. I first created my marketing budget (easy to do when you're paying with plastic). I added as an expense to the budget salaries for a sales team (not just one representative), benefits, training, marketing materials, and sales giveaways. I also added a bonus structure and monthly rewards for employees who referred their friends or family members to our agency.

You might be saying right now, "Budgeting? Are you kidding me? I have no clue how my account comes up with a sales budget, and it never makes any sense to me." Have a private session with me, and I will teach you budgeting in plain English. It will be the best money you ever spend, and the return on investment will be at least a 10 percent change in your profit margin. I say that so confidently because I have been able to prove it time and time again at agency after agency that has called me in to do a financial review. That's how I got my nickname—the "Solutionist."

Next, I put an ad in the paper for a physician liaison or, in other words, a sales representative. (You have no clue how relevant the title you give your sales rep truly is.) I interviewed ten representatives, and each one had to have one thing in common: he or she had to have experienced or witnessed a family member who benefited from home care or hospice services. Of course, other qualities are important, such as communication skills, prior sales success, and an eagerness to learn. However, if a sales representative has all these qualities but also fifteen facial earrings and purple hair, you need to continue looking. Unfortunately, most of the world doesn't want to deal with a sales representative who looks like an advertisement for staples.

Then, once again, I tortured my extraordinary husband by telling him I wanted to do the hiring, training, managing, and budgeting without him being involved. I know this sounds mean, but my husband had no trust in sales representatives. We had representatives when we first opened our business. We grew for the first couple of years, even though we fired all of them in less than a year. Bill found them at home when they were supposed to be at our booth, which we paid $3,000 for, at a senior expo. His distrust couldn't be shaken. I knew this was one of those projects I had to tackle alone. He agreed to let me have what I asked for. said he believed in me and trusted me. In exchange, he wanted me to give him monthly reports to keep him and the board informed about our progress. When my husband asks for monthly reports, that means every dollar spent must have a return on investment. My husband knew the direct cost of every service that our agency provided. He would be able to calculate exactly how many referrals each patient liaison would have to bring in to cover his or her salary, so I knew I couldn't pull the wool over his eyes.

I also knew that having someone like that to keep me accountable would force me to collect data and not slack off. I was so lucky to have someone believe in me. I knew even if I failed, I would still be loved by this amazing man.

Once I had his approval, I started interviewing. Then I took another incredibly crazy risk: instead of hiring one sales representative, I hired three. I did so because when I started my step one study, I found out that I truly needed three representatives to reclaim my market share.

Next, I signed us all up to attend a boot camp for sales training for their first week of work. Yes, I took brand-new sales representatives who had never sold for the home care and hospice industry to a sales boot camp during their first week of work with my struggling company. I chose the boot camp that I thought would train the sales representatives not only how to sell but how to navigate Medicare regulations for home care, hospice, and private duty organizations. Even private duty-only agencies need to know Medicare regulations. You need to know the rules of the other service lines so that you can develop your unique selling points. You need to make sure you are approaching these other organizations with ideas that fit their conditions of participation.

I was particularly selective with my hiring. I had to have sales representatives who understood what my agency provided to people. I needed representatives who had seen a family member benefit from home care or hospice in some way so he or she would have a personal connection to the industry. I interviewed twenty representatives, and brought in three for a second interview with my husband for his opinion on my decision. I needed his analytical eye, as I was genuinely beginning to feel the weight of my risk. I needed my husband to re-interview my selections. I needed his critical eye to give me a thumb's up. He agreed on all three of them. The team and I were off to our sales training.

4

Our Journey Begins

TWO OF THE REPRESENTATIVES MET THEIR new boss at the airport an hour before the flight. They had never even met each other, but together we set out on our journey. The third representative couldn't attend the training because of the short notice and family obligations. I remember telling them before we got on the flight how I was risking my entire future on this sales team. We would either be victorious and proud of saving everyone's jobs at Immediate, or we would all be out looking for employment. I said I wanted to succeed, and that is why I wanted to give them the tools they needed to succeed. They were both committed to the mission.

We went to the boot camp, purchased the guru's software to manage our accounts, and returned home with a lot of work to do. We had a clearly defined mission, a positive attitude, and a clear goal in mind. I knew I had chosen the right team after getting to know them over the three days. I will always be thankful for my team. I was the luckiest person in the world to find these individuals. Ronald Young and Steve Pesature, I am forever grateful. You are heroes in disguise.

In the coming chapters, I will share how I took all the information I learned from the sales training, books, and processes that I studied and made them into a five-step plan that saved my business. Our company was transformed from one that was failing to one that made a six-figure profit the first year after its sales team was launched in January 2010.

All our sales techniques were 100 percent legal, according to all anti-kickback laws and Stark II laws. I have been able to replicate my sales process and success at other companies. I have taken agencies from start-up to incredible growth their first year. I have helped mature agencies, which were like mine, get out of the red. Creating a culture of sales has been some of the most satisfying work I have ever done. I am now not just making sure that my agency is servicing as many patients as we can; I'm also contributing to providing services for patients around the country. I have met and worked with some incredible people. I am so blessed to be their business associate. Come with me as I take you through the five steps to sales success.

5

The First Step: Study

Many of us remember having to prepare for a big test. We would be up studying all night so that we could get a decent grade. Some of us would make index cards, and some would just read the chapters over and over again.

But none of us could even begin to prepare without knowing what the test would cover. We needed to know which chapters to study. We needed a study guide. We needed to know what vocabulary we had to be familiar with in order to study the chapter. Well, with sales, it's the same approach.

For a minute, let's pretend we are selling cars. We live on a deserted island with nine other neighbors. Seven of us have driver's licenses. One of the seven has a family car and a fun car (not the minivan) for date nights with his wife. One has a work vehicle and a home vehicle. A total of nine cars are being used on the island. If I open up a car dealership and stock one hundred cars, I am never going to sell them. Remember, the island is isolated. No other states where I can sell cars are nearby. I have no other dealerships I can trade with, so I'm stuck with these cars. Knowing the potential customers available to use your services is why you should do feasibility studies. A good one will include market research data. A feasibility study evaluates a project's potential for success.

One of my clients wanted to open a hospice in a very small community in Pennsylvania. The feasibility study showed that the area had fewer than five deaths per month, and two large hospices already covered the area. Of all the deaths that occurred in this area, two were unexpected deaths and wouldn't have been on hospice services. God himself could not sell enough hospice services in this area to keep the company viable. Be cautious when selecting where you want to open your business. A company called Health Market Science conducts feasibility studies. In fact, they provide my CRM company with market share data that allows us to select our targets. The next most common mistake is our vision of what sales or marketers do to bring in business.

Many of my clients started off with this kind of system: they grabbed someone they met and paid him or her $10 to drop off brochures in doctors' offices. *We are selling services*, not pizzas.

In fact, we aren't truly selling anything. We are helping to identify every person who is eligible for services to allow that person to have a better life. That's right: we are life changers. If you are going to pay someone to drop off brochures, you might as well as provide them with a branded trash bag too.

When I was a full-time nurse doing home care visits, one of my favorite things was to see a patient reach his or her goal. I would ask every patient, "What is your goal in receiving home care services?" Their goals never matched my nursing care plans. Their goals were personal. Some would say, "I want to be able to see my grandson play soccer again." Others would say, "I want to visit my home country one more time before I die." I tell you this so you can see the value in the service.

One thing that truly sets me apart from other consultants is that I was a full-time home care nurse for three years before opening my agency. Many organizations today continue to struggle to get the clinical and financial sides of the business to work for the common goal of the patient. At my organization, this was just a core value. Everyone was reminded at every meeting that every decision we made ultimately affected a human being. Accordingly, unique experiences were immediately transferred to my sales team. When my organization opened our Well Mom Well Baby (WMWB) program, I was the RN who went first to be trained on conducting postpartum and newborn assessment.

I mentioned before that I had a unique childhood. During my life, many seniors have either lived with my family or spent the day with my mom. My great-grandma suffered from Alzheimer's. She would cure any ailment you had as a child with cream cheese dip, potato chips, and a Coke. My great-aunt Cecelia was funny and loving. She would call everyone "little darling," and when she got mad, she would say "hell's bells." She taught me manners. My parents, of course, taught me manners, but Aunt Cecelia was diligent in demonstrating kindness and manners. Then we had my grandmother, but I was not yet three when she died, so I don't remember her. We had my cousin Sherry, who was staying with us to receive chemo at the local cancer center. We had my grandfather, who was one of my best friends. He came to work with me every day when I started the home care agency. As you can see, I didn't choose to be a caregiver. I was born to be a caregiver.

I made this experience of being raised in a home that had many seniors who needed caregiving my agency's core value. This life experience was part of every hiring decision and every financial decision. If an aide came in to be hired for a job, in my mind, I was sending her to my childhood home with all those vulnerable adults. That home consisted of a loving caregiver with three children and a husband who worked full-time. If I wouldn't let you into that home, then I would not let you into someone else's home either. I mention this to you because, when you start to study your data, your life experiences and biases are quite important in how you will view that data.

If you are just beginning, your need to study is different from an organization that already has a home care agency or hospice. New organizations need to know who is providing the services in the current market. How many seniors are in your area, and how many of them have used home care services? Having this research data will let you determine how saturated the market is. Market share data can be purchased from someone who aggregates claims. For many investors or businesspeople, this is how they open a business. They find an area that has a need, build a building, hire people looking for a job, and open their agency. If they put it in the right spot, they may make it.

Well, I did none of the studying I just mentioned. I didn't care about the competition. I knew that my life experiences would create a culture of nurses who all truly loved home care as much as I did. I wasn't worried about the size of the organization because I had no investment company. The business grew so fast from 1995 to 1996 that we had to move out of our house and rent office space. My husband and I worked the first five years without a day off. I'm serious; we worked every holiday for five years. In 2002, we outgrew that building, and bought and moved into a larger building. I was the sales department, and yet we grew and grew.

My husband and I were so busy running the day-to-day duties of the agency that I was no longer able to make any sales calls. The next four years was a crazy time. We had three more children and now had five children under the age of ten. We were the intake desk, scheduler, nurse recruiters, human resources, payroll, authorization, and billing. Finally, about 2000, we were able to hire staff to help us, and we started to breathe. My sister, God bless her, was with me from day one. We couldn't have done what we did without her. Denise, I love you!

Then, early in 2009, we met with our accountant to review the 2008 cost report and learned that we had suffered a loss—our cost had increased and our volume had decreased. The market shifted, and we had a lot less Medicare revenue. We had a lot of new contracts that we took on for low gross profit margins, but we were hoping that the volume would be there to offset the margins. We did nothing and just thought this would change for 2009. That's exactly what happened. That year 2009 was our second year of a loss, and it was more than $180,000. After the first quarter of 2010, we met with our finance committee. They projected that 2010 was going to be our largest loss, and that we couldn't financially sustain the company in 2011 without a dramatic change in revenue.

The fear I mentioned earlier appeared in 2009, and the sales team was born. Now it was time to study my data. So where do you begin?

First, look at every referral you received over the last year. Study your referral log or admission report and look to see who called or faxed in the referral. Make a list of the data. We started by analyzing data from 2009. Start with January, and go day to day. As you review, you will have several referrals from the same person. If that happens, list all these under his or her name. Sorting this data is the creation of your account list.

To define an account, I will use the visualization that my CRM company taught me. It is the physical location of the place giving you the referral. Using this definition, a hospital, nursing home, assisted living facility, doctor's office, senior center, adult day care, or dialysis center would each be an account. You may need to google the actual name of a physician's practice. Several physicians often all work at one organization, and they have a group name. See Exhibit 1 for an example of the spreadsheet that I used to do my aggregation of referrals.

Exhibit 1

Patients Name	Date of Referral	Start of Care Date	Non Admit Date	Referred by (Account Name)

When I did this the first time, I learned that I had six hospitals in my area that referred between one and seven patients a month. I also had several physicians' offices that referred from one to three patients a month. I made the names of the hospital the account names. The name of the physician's practice (e.g., Trevose Family Practice) was an account name, and the physicians and their secretary were the contacts under the account. See Exhibit 2 for an example of the spreadsheet I used to do my aggregation of accounts. Therefore, the first part of Step One is to review your current referrals to help identify how many accounts your organization currently has referred to your organization.

Exhibit 2

Account	July	August	Sept	Monthly Average
Elkins Park Medical				
Episcopal Hospital				
Ekison's Living				
Employee Referral				
Esperanza 5th				
Esperanza 6th				

Then we did the same thing for 2008 and 2007. I was shocked at what I saw happen to the accounts from year to year. Those that had referred from seven to nine patients a month from 2007 were not referring at all now. We went from thirty-five accounts referring in 2007 to seventeen accounts referring. Why? What had happened?

Next, we performed a SWOT (Strengths, Weaknesses, Opportunities, and Threats) analysis. SWOT is a document you can download from Google. This tool is an overall strategic assessment of the business. We would use this later when we would develop the unique selling points of the organization. We noticed that some accounts referred a lot, and other accounts barely referred at all. We now had to decide how to classify the accounts from the ones that were the highest referring to the less important.

6

The Second Step: Accounts and Accountability

AFTER WE HAD ALL THE DATA, WE SORTED the accounts in order of most referrals to least referrals. Next, we separated them into four groups. The accounts that had the most referrals were the top 25 percent, and we labeled that group A accounts. The next highest referring group we labeled B accounts. We made the top referring accounts A, then B, C, and finally D accounts (D accounts we only received one referral from during the three years). In order to be called an A account, the account had to refer more than nine patients over the previous ninety days. To be a B account, they had to refer between five and nine patients over the previous ninety days. To be a C account, they had to refer between one and four patients over the last ninety days. You need to follow the same process for your data to clearly see what is going on at your agency. Data needs to be reviewed every quarter.

We then added the ZIP codes to the list, and separated the accounts into territories that each sales representative would be assigned to market. Each sales representative can handle a maximum of forty accounts. If you already have forty accounts in the territory that you want to grow in, you need more than one marketer. In fact, I would recommend that each sales representative be given no more than twenty accounts that have already referred. You need to leave room for them to prospect new accounts and grow your organization. If you are splitting the territory, make sure you record which ZIP codes belong to each sales representative. Share that list with your intake staff and clinical staff.

Next, document which clinical staff work in that territory and list their contact information and status. Now you need to make your sales representatives truly understand the services that your organization provides. You can do this by sending them out into the field with your clinical staff and watch the clinical staff provide hands-on services to your clients. I wanted my sales representatives to be able to see patients receiving services. I wanted them to discuss what home care meant to the patient so that they could have an understanding from the patient's point of view. Observing and talking to a patient showed them that they were not only sales representatives; they also helped each potential referral source identify patients they could refer. They were able to see that they were helping patients change their lives for the better. With this type of perspective, they are no longer salespeople. Knowing that they are helping people receive needed help gives them the confidence to ask for a referral. They are asking to provide a service that can change patients' lives.

I also wanted a relationship between the liaisons and the field staff. Our clinical visiting staff are paid per visit. Our sales team liked that because the nurse was paid if he or she could see the patient. The sales team knew that the clinical staff would exhaust all efforts to see the patients. They would only be paid if they turned each referral into an admission. This built trust between the representatives and the sales team.

Next, I made the clinical team go out for a day with a sales representative. Watching the sales representative work showed the clinical staff how difficult it is to build and maintain a relationship with accounts. Their joint visits allowed the clinical staff to give a brief report on the patients from an account. Joint visits were the smartest thing we did. They taught the clinical staff how quickly an account can go bad if they don't communicate with them.

Next, I clearly defined my expectations of visit frequency to each account based on how the account was rated. The A accounts and B accounts were scheduled to be seen weekly. We wanted to make sure that another company couldn't capture that market share. The C accounts we put on the schedule based on the account's referral potential. If an account was a C account, could it become a B or an A account? If it had the patient volume to support a transition to a higher rated account, then we saw that account weekly as well. If an account would never be more than a C account, the account's location determined if it would be seen weekly, but most were scheduled for semimonthly or monthly visits.

When we started to map the accounts into a schedule for sales representative visits, some of the representatives had twenty accounts to visit each week. They then created lists of the next twenty accounts they would prospect. Some representatives have a hard time doing this, and others can be done in ten minutes. If the hospital in their area isn't on their current list of accounts, then that is one type of account you want them to prospect weekly. I know many of you are wondering why I would have them waste their time at a hospital with its own home care agency. If you look at the health market science data, you will see that most hospitals with their own home care agencies capture only about 40 percent to 55 percent of the patients referred for home care. Now there are many reasons for this. They may not service the area that the discharged patient is going to. They may not take the patient's insurance. They may have a staffing issue in that area and need to refer the patient to another provider. The physician, patient, or caregiver may want them serviced by another company that they know. Hospitals have the highest utilization of our services by far. Every hospital, with few exceptions, gives my agency between three and sixty referrals a month. Hospitals can give you at least a few a month, if not more.

Many of you have said that you can't get into the hospital system. They won't let you in the hospital. Then you need to find a network partner. Your agency has companies that it currently works with or refers to; those companies may have sales representatives who have relationships within that hospital. You need to find that connection. Ask the sales representative to take you into the hospital on his or her next visit so you can be introduced. Why would another sales representative do that? Because you are going to take that sales representative to your best accounts and introduce him or her. You need to visit these accounts together at least four times; then you will have access to go alone because you will know how the system works. Make sure you find a network partner that is selling to your same audience. This includes businesses that sell DME (durable medical equipment), pharmaceuticals, oxygen supplies, beds, nutritional supplements, or diapers. Find your way in. It's right there in front of you. Trust me.

The next type of provider with a high number of discharges is the rehab facility. Add these facilities to your list if they are not currently referring patients to your organization. Rehab facilities have the next largest number of patients to refer to your organization. Many sales representatives want to start listing doctors' offices. Why? They're easier. You can convert most doctors' offices to referring accounts in less than ninety days. It takes about six months to get a rehab facility to refer to you. But the bigger account has more volume. Let's look at a comparison.

Month	MD	Rehab	Hospital	
January	0	0	0	
February	0	0	0	
March	1	0	0	
April	0	0	0	
May	1	0	0	
June	1	2	0	
July	1	3	0	
August	2	4	0	
September	1	4	0	
October	1	5	0	
November	1	5	0	
December	2	4	5	
Total	11	27	5	1 Year
January	1	5	7	
February	1	5	9	
March	2	5	7	
April	2	6	7	
May	2	6	7	
June	2	7	7	
July	2	6	7	
August	2	6	8	
September	2	6	8	
October	2	6	8	
November	2	6	8	
December	2	6	8	
Total	22	70	91	2 Year

During the first year, your rehab facilities will probably be your A accounts. By the second year, however, those A accounts are bumped down by the hospital accounts. I've seen this happen over and over again. Invest the time to see the hospital accounts. Once you're in, you are in for life.

If you still have room on your list, add a few skilled nursing facilities if you have private duty or hospice. Assisted living facilities and whole life communities should also be on the list. Next you need to go to doctors' offices. Don't just let your sales representatives drive around, walk in, and do a cold call. Call the office first and ask who in the organization handles home care and hospice referrals. If the person says the office doesn't refer, hang up and call the next one on your list. If the person tells you the name, document it because you will need it when you stop in to make your first visit. Keep calling until your calendar is full. You need to see between thirty-five and forty a week; how many you visit each day is your choice as long as they are all done.

Remember that done isn't done just because you went to see the account and maybe even got a referral. You did nothing that day if you don't document what you did. I am going to tell you a true story about Steve, one of my sales representatives whom I just love. Well, I love all of you: Ron, Margaret, Terry, Abdul, and Venessa.

Steve had gotten to the point of consistently making his bonuses after about eighteen months at the agency. But Steve had to go on leave for eight weeks to have bilateral knee replacements. Thank God he had such great documentation because my other sales representatives could view his account notes. They could look to see who Steve dealt with at each of his top accounts, and see them to keep those accounts maintained. When Steve came back, yes his accounts were down a little, but within two months, Steve had once again reclaimed his stake. And he didn't have to beg or give out expensive, illegal gifts. He just had to help them visualize every patient who needed the services.

Now the sales representatives went out selling. We used *Top 20 Selling* by Michael Giudicissi as our bible at my organization—and thank God we did. My staff was able to build account after account. They quickly developed their top twenty accounts and continued to build and build. Today, every rep who works for my agency easily makes his or her monthly and quarterly bonuses. It's amazing when you first start a sales department with a few house accounts, and see your reps keep increasing the number of accounts that refer to them. Within two years, one of my reps had more than fifty accounts that referred to him. Document the number of accounts, and your weekly expectations, rating, scheduling, and accountability.

7

Step Three: Lead

WHAT IS LEADERSHIP? MORE importantly, what does leadership mean to me? I wanted to be a leader who could remove all emotions from managing employees and yet be quite close with my staff. Books that I read said this isn't possible, and don't be friends with your staff because it's too hard to discipline them if they aren't doing their jobs. No matter what the experts out there had to say, I couldn't change from being Cheryl. I had to find a way to be their friend, boss, leader, teacher, and disciplinarian, Cheryl style. I've had to fire a couple of people over my twenty years in management, and it's never fun. But I have made it doable for me and my leaders. If you have clearly defined your expectations, given them the knowledge and tools to meet those expectations, and then measured and shared their results with them, it is much easier.

When I met with a staff member to review what was happening, I would pull out a form that I complete for my staff every month and review the results. The individual either did or did not meet my expectations. It's not about liking the person. There is no partiality because it's about numbers. Numbers remove emotions, and every three months the manager needs to meet with each sales representative to evaluate the numbers. We would also update our admission goal every month at that meeting. The image below is what our usual agenda would include.

We had a biweekly newsletter that went out to every employee and subcontractor working with our organization. We included all our sales stats for everyone to see. Tracking admissions sent the message to try to get every qualified patient admitted. This let everyone know that non-admits were being tracked.

Every quarter, I would meet with each sales representative one on one. At that meeting, we would review each account's current rating and compare it with the previous quarter. We would see how many accounts referred and how many of those accounts were of each type—hospitals, rehabs, doctors' offices, or senior communities. Sales managers should know the contacts of all of the A accounts. I suggest that you go out with your reps each quarter to visit these accounts, and reach out to them by phone or email monthly. I also would connect with each of the contacts on LinkedIn.

I would post our company's unique selling points the same weeks that the sales reps were out delivering the messages. I would get comments back from some of the contacts, for example, "Yes, Steve just showed us your amazing 'Beat Goes On' Program!" The most important thing that I had to do as their leader was give them a reason to see each account each week. Now let me explain what I mean by unique selling points and how I created them.

First, I asked several of my top clinicians to come in for a brainstorming session. I started the meeting the same way that I usually started every marketing meeting: by walking in with loud, fun music playing on my iPhone. Next, I reminded all employees that all meetings still start with today, to remember whom we work for, and make every decision with that patient and his or her family in mind. Then I simply went around the room and asked some questions, such as "Tell me about one of the proudest moments you experienced working with any patient, referral source, or family member." They each told me some amazing stories. Some brought tears to my eyes.

One nurse told us that she was on call one weekend, and a patient called, saying she had just come home from the hospital and didn't know how to use the kangaroo feeding pump. The nurse said, "No problem. I will be there in thirty minutes." When she arrived at the patient's house, the patient and her daughter said, "Now I know why they call your company Immediate Homecare." We turned this into one of our unique selling points (USPs). We all went around the room and spoke about what Immediate meant to them. What could we do differently from our competition to connect with the company's name? We wrote out the new expectations and processes. We then discussed what the sales message would have to be for each account type. How would we sell this to the hospital discharge planners, rehab facilities, skilled nursing facilities, assisted living facilities, physicians' offices, and senior audiences? We developed a script for the sales team for each account type. We continued this process several times until we came up with twelve USPs. Some of these involved physician groups of specialists.

Our "Beat Goes On" program was done with cardiologists. Our diabetes program, "Put the Diet Back into Diabetes," was developed with endocrinologists, and our "Breathe Program" was done with a nurse practitioner who had experience with chronic obstructive pulmonary disease (COPD). I wrote all the programs myself and had them copyrighted. Now

I sell the programs for $1,000, and agencies all over the country use them to help decrease their emergent care for hospitalization rates. Some of our programs were built on skills that our staff had, such as wound care certification, Spanish speaking, or end of life care certification. These skills contributed to the organization's USPs, such as our wound care program, palliative care, and the creation of a whole Spanish team.

Once USPs were prepared, we created branded flyers and posters for each of our unique selling points. We held training sessions with all our staff to inform them of our programs. We also added the USPs to our orientation program. Then I had the best idea. I decided to schedule each USP on a calendar. We tried to schedule ones that were diagnosis specific to occur during the months dedicated to awareness of that diagnosis. We scheduled the USPs to run every two weeks. We ran our USPs every other week for several reasons.

1. If we didn't get in to see an account one week, we would get to it next week.

2. If you only see two accounts a month, you would get to cover each USP.

3. It would make visits to the accounts not always about teaching something.

We would alternate the purpose of the visits to see each account. If we were seeing the accounts four times a month, we needed to have four reasons to see them. Two of the visits would be to help identify patients who would qualify and benefit from our USP, but what would we do the other two weeks? I went back to some of my sales bibles to find some motivation.

Most of those books said that your sales representative must be someone who makes each account encounter fun. They need to include fun in some of their visits to their accounts. Otherwise, an account visit may cause the contact person to try to hide. So how could we make it fun? What would make that person stop what he or she was doing and go out to say "Hi" for just a minute? I thought about the representatives that I did take time out of my day to see. What were they doing? One had a joke every time he came in, as well as a promotional item. With others, it was either food or a small gift for my desk, and I usually wanted to get mine.

We knew we needed small promotional giveaways to leave at the accounts. We knew we had to stay within the law when we were selecting items. Most cost less than a dollar. We again got together with the group and came up with twelve items. Give your team a budget amount, and let the entire team get together to approve the items. There is nothing worse than a rep not wanting to give out a giveaway that the company purchased. We also rotated the items that we gave away from ones that were disposable but fun to ones that could be used multiple times. Disposable items helped keep the cost down and still added fun to the experience. We had stickers branded with our company's logo and colors, and had some cute expressions on them.

1. S'mores granola bars: "We are ready for s'more referrals."

2. Mints: "Your referrals are worth a mint."

3. Gum: We chose Extra brand gum, and the sticker said, "We will go the extra mile for your patients."

4. Popcorn: "Pop your next referral my way."

5. Life Savers: "We can be a life saver! Call us when you need to be rescued!"

6. Hot chocolate mix: "If chocolate doesn't solve it, call us."

Giving out the branded items was fun. When I went out with my reps to observe them in the field, so many contacts commented on how they loved our corny giveaways. Discharge planners would say, "Cheryl, on the busiest, most hectic days, my rep from Immediate would show up; they saw how busy we were, so they just stayed for three minutes, brightened the room, changed the mood, and picked up their referrals." What excited me the most about that comment was when she said "my sales rep." She truly felt that my company's representative was her business partner. Here is a list of our promotional items.

Day	Promotional Giveaway
1/3/2022	Pens
2/2/2022	Granola Bar's
3/4/2022	Paper Caddy
4/3/2022	Mints
5/3/2022	Highlighters
6/2/2022	gum
7/2/2022	sun screen
8/1/2022	popcorn
8/31/2022	first aide kit
9/30/2022	Life Savers
10/30/2022	Post It Notes
11/29/2022	Hot Chocolate
12/29/2022	Ice Scrappers

We scheduled the giveaways into the calendar, and only had one week most months when we needed to think of something else fun.

We wanted them to be unique, things that others weren't doing. I remembered from one of the gurus the idea of crossword puzzle handouts. I thought about having the contacts at the account complete a crossword puzzle tied to the USPs for that month. Whoever wanted to fill it out would fax it to the agency; each month, we would select one winner of a $25 gift card. On the form, they would include their contact information, which was great because we had their email addresses. We added their email addresses into PlayMaker, and our CRM would be able to email them thank you notes or patient updates. We also had a separate crossword puzzle raffle for our staff with a $25 gift card prize. This crossword puzzle reminded the staff of the USPs and expectations, and made them all sales savvy. Finally, my fifty-two-week calendar was done. I knew that when my sales representative walked into an account and the gatekeeper said that Steve was there, they would all come out of their offices to say hello and see what he had that week. It's simple when you have a plan.

Then I asked myself if I were a sales rep, what other tools would I need besides the obvious business cards, phone, and brochures all branded correctly and professionally? I asked all sales representatives to tell me what tool I hadn't provided that they would need to be successful. The sales representatives wanted a contact resource management system. We looked at several and choose PlayMaker CRM. The software included Health Market Science data for each hospital, nursing home, and physician's office. With this information, we could easily see which doctors we should target. We were almost ready to go. I just had to define my expectations clearly. Again, it was time to bring the sales team together to develop expectations and rewards for excellence. On to the next step.

8

Expectations and Excellence

ONE OF THE FAILURES OF LEADERS delegating responsibilities is not making the desired outcomes explicit. A saying attributed to Michelangelo is, "The greater danger for most of us lies not in setting our aim so high that we miss it, but in setting our aim so low that we reach it." Bring the team together and ask them to help create expectations, goals, and rewards. How many face-to-face visits a week can their sales team do? How many accounts do you want them to manage? They may say they can handle one hundred accounts without any problems, but bring them back your way of thinking by saying, "You know what? Studies show that building a relationship and getting an account to know, and trust you is how you get referrals." Studies say you need to see accounts each week to build a relationship. Have them fill out their daily call schedules to see just how many accounts they have to see each week.

Once you have all their currently referring accounts scheduled, you can see how many prospects can be added to fill up their schedules. Now they can manage their schedules more effectively. We only want a rep to handle up to forty accounts. This means each rep should only have thirty to leave room for prospecting. Knowing this information is how you determine how many representatives your company truly needs. I caution you to also know your staffing levels in territories before you hire a sales rep to sell your care. No sales rep wants to get a first referral only to be told the company can't take the referral because the only nurse in that area is on vacation.

Next, we discussed what types of accounts I wanted them to pursue. Remember that if you just send them to rehab centers and hospitals, you may not get a referral for six months. Most reps will quit by that time because they feel like failures. You have to mix the account types so that they can get some immediate success. Next, you need to teach documentation requirements and timelines, expenses, and admit goals. Each representative would need to prospect a minimum of ten new accounts. He or she would prospect for a maximum number of weekly visits to an account that could refer at least three patients a month. If he or she didn't convert a prospect to a referring account by two weeks before the last visit, the rep had to call me to discuss the account. I had to see if I could help reps convert prospects to referring accounts or if they should have more time to work the accounts. Sometimes it was time to move on.

We decided that we would do a maximum of twelve weekly visits to doctors' offices, at most twenty-six visits to rehab centers or assisted living facilities, and a maximum of fifty-two weekly visits to hospitals. We also clearly crafted a plan on how to get the hospitals to build that account. I typed up the expectations and goals and posted them directly into their CRM so that they could refer to them at any time. Below is the required number of weekly visits and goals by type of account.

Expectation Document	Goal
Sales Contacts Per Wk Rquired	40-50
Qualify: Account is willing/able to ref	5
Prospecting- Account is qualified but hasn't referred	10
Maintenance- Account refers monthly	15
Community Education: Health Matter talks	4
Visiting Hospitalized Patients- Hospital qualifing	7
Total	41

Frequency to visit account by rating	
A accounts (Top 25 % of referring)	1-5 times a week
B accounts (2nd 25% of referring accounts)	1 week
c accounts (accounts that can't refer 1 a month)	Monthly
Prospecting Accounts see for 11 weeks then do reveal	1 week
Reveal/Tell Call done after 11 weeks of prospecting	1 quarterly

Week	Date	Unique Selling Point (USP)	Common Objections	Review Expectations	#Sales Calls Previous week	Types of sales calls	# of Admits	# of Non Admits
1								
2								
3								
4								
5								
6								
7								
8								
9								
10								

The leader need not have all the answers. The leader's role is to ensure that the process for setting the expectations is followed. You and the person(s) accepting the responsibility should build in from the beginning some agreeable method for routinely reporting progress. Send your report to them each week. I use a CRM for this part. Shown below is a sample of what I would send them each week so that they could see their progress.

Next, we decided when a sales representative would be eligible for a bonus. We created our sales bonus structure from a purely financial point of view. I knew that I wanted each representative to make the agency $100,000 in profit. I added it to the cost of the sales representative's salary, plus all of that rep's costs, taxes, insurance, benefits, and monthly expense budgets. When I added these numbers, it was up to $570,000. Next, I looked to see what percentage I wanted direct cost, what percentage would pay indirect cost, and what percentage I wanted to have as a profit. I used national numbers for like providers. I had my accountant help and came up with a bonus that wouldn't be paid until the rep brought in twenty admissions for the home health side. A hospice patient had a shared value of 2.5 because the average hospice patient's revenue was 2.5 times that of the average Medicare patient. So the admission goal for hospice was set at eight per month. For private pay, the amount was based on hours or days sold.

Many organizations don't pay a bonus for admissions. I think that's a big mistake. All my employees are given business cards, and if they refer friends or family members, they can receive $50. An employee referral is one of my A accounts. You need to make sure that in your referral bonus structure, you clearly define when a bonus is paid and what constitutes a bonus-eligible referral. You need to clearly define non-admissions and readmissions, and record and report this data for every single referral that comes in your door to the sales representatives every month at their sales management meeting.

A Medicare patient who had only three visits becomes a LUPA, so he or she may not be given full credit or a private duty case that only gets one day for a family member to go out for three hours, or a hospice patient who dies within the first three days. A LUPA is a low utilization patient and Medicare will not pay you for the episode but pay your per visit. You need to put some parameters in place before a patient's admission would qualify a sales rep for a bonus. For example, you can't pay a bonus on a Medicare patient who only receives four visits and becomes a LUPA. You also can't pay a bonus on a hospice patient who dies within four days. Five became our magic number. In order for the sales rep to qualify for a bonus, the patient needed to have five home health visits or receive hospice services for at least five days. I also do not believe in paying bonuses for the length of stay on hospice. That's asking for fraudulent referrals. You can have a bonus structure, but you better make sure you also have staff with strong qualifying abilities and a corporate compliance plan in place.

9

Success

VINCE LOMBARDI SAID IT BEST: "THE ONLY place success comes before work is in the dictionary." This is so true. It takes a lot of hard work to get to this point. Reflecting back, I wish that I had developed a sales team from day one. I wish I didn't feel that sales was an expense. I thought we couldn't afford to have sales reps in the beginning. I ended up working five years straight because I didn't make enough revenue to hire the staff that I truly needed. Well, better late than never. We went from three consecutive years of loss to a profit of more than $300,000 the first year we started our sales team. That same year, I added $570,000 to the company's budget for sales and marketing. We increased revenue by $2,000,000, even with five times more competition in our market. We also had to deal with our Medicare patients in our area switching to Medicare Advantage Plans. Every year, the percentage of patients we served who had traditional Medicare decreased. In 2010, we had the lowest number of Medicare patients serviced at only 20 percent; yet, we still made this profit, and I was the sales manager. I had never sold a thing my entire life. I had never taken one college course for sales or marketing. But using what I learned from the five gurus, the thousands of books that I read, fear as my motivator, and my unique fifty-two-week plan, we did it.

Since 2010, my agency has doubled in size. At the end of 2009, we had fifty employees; by 2013, we had one hundred. Only three employees, besides the sales reps, were added to the GA budget. The rest were all clinicians or direct care workers. How was I able to do that? First was to provide tools to streamline office processes: email faxing services, better technology, computers, monitors, and software. You should find something that will improve the office atmosphere. We also adopted a customer service culture and the FISH! philosophy.

What is the FISH! philosophy? It includes four simple, interconnected practices.

1. **Be There:** When people need you, they need all of you. Setting aside distractions and judgments to be fully

present is a sign of respect. It improves communication and strengthens relationships.

2. **Play:** You can be serious about your work without taking yourself so seriously. Play is a mindset more than a specific activity. It allows you to throw yourself with enthusiasm and creativity into whatever you are doing in a way that is natural, not forced. "Playing" with ideas helps you find solutions to everyday challenges.

3. **Make Their Day:** Simple gestures of thoughtfulness, thanks, and recognition make people feel appreciated and valued. When you make someone else feel good, you feel good too.

4. **Choose Your Attitude:** To actually choose how you respond to life, not just react, you must be intentional. When you get up, decide who you want to be today. Moment-to-moment awareness is key. Ask yourself throughout the day, "What is my attitude right now? Is it helping the people who depend on me? Is it helping me to be most effective?"[1]

Through the FISH! philosophy, we build stronger relationships with the team members we work with, the customers we

---

[1] "What is FISH!?", FISH, accessed May 2, 2022, https://www.fishphilosophy.com/what-is-fish/

serve, the students we teach, and the people we love. We have monthly FISH meetings, which really keeps our culture of sales strong.

Other things to improve work culture and celebrate success were also added. We have theme days and monthly birthday celebrations; we provide the cake, and employees come together to sing happy birthday to everyone celebrating that month. We also allow them to decorate their workstations and give them an opportunity to express their needs in monthly management meetings.

Make sure you have a meeting of managers to bring suggestions for streamlining processes. These are positive meetings and not sessions for complaining. Provide managers with gift cards they can use to reward employees for hard work. Have a year-end state of the union to share your data and announce the next year's goals, and then return to Step One. Make sure that every employee knows that the customer pays him or her, not the owner. The owner only handles the money.

10

Maintain Success

GO BACK TO THE DATA YOU AGGREGATED when you were on Step One. Compare the previous quarter's data to the current data. How many accounts were referring to your organization, and has the number grown quarterly? How many accounts does each sales rep have referring to your organization, and has the number grown? What account types (A, B, C, and prospecting) per rep were referring, and how has that changed? You will see that some accounts will evolve from D accounts to C, B, or even A accounts. You will see that every quarter, your revenue is growing. You also want to measure your revenue streams by service line.

Other areas that must be measured at least quarterly are your staffing levels and turnover rate. If your turnover rate is high, you have one of two problems: a poor orientation program and support system in place for new employees, or a manager issue. Today, I see this all the time. I offer to train company administrators, CEOs, or clinical management staff at my agency for two days. I will ask them what I ask every potential customer: "Did you hire for skill and not personality?" So many organizations will hire a manager who has many skills, as evidenced by multiple letters behind their names, but who has zero personality. I can't make that manager any better by spending two days with him or her. You need to hire a manager who has a personality and most of the skills you need. You can teach the other skills.

You also need to study your company's publicly reported outcomes. This information should be made into a chart and shared with all staff each quarter. This is also something that can be a company USP. You need to look at the complaints. These provide useful feedback for agencies to identify their weaknesses. Unless you are aware of customer dissatisfaction or unhappiness, you may find it difficult to address your shortcomings. If you don't study your complaints and address the issues as opportunities for improvement, things will not only remain unchanged but they are also more likely to worsen. I appreciate customers who take the trouble to complain about deplorable service. By studying your complaints, you know what staff education needs to be added, and which employees may need to be coached with customer service training classes.

We have a policy that if a patient calls in with a complaint, the call goes directly to one of the supervisors. We don't want the patient to have to tell the story twice. Also, always listen and apologize by saying, "We are sorry that we didn't meet your expectations." We offer a solution to meet the patient's expectations and make the changes immediately—and then we add the wow. We ask if we can treat the patient to a pizza for taking the time to help us improve a future patient's experience. This really shocks the person.

My sales rep came in one day and said that the discharge planner at the hospital had a patient complaint to tell him about. I immediately stopped what I was doing and asked what happened. The sales rep started laughing. He said the discharge planner told him Mr. Z was a patient who had Immediate before. The discharge planner went into Mr. Z's room to tell Mr. Z he was referring him back to Immediate. Mr. Z responded, "Yes, I had them before, but I had to complain to them." When the discharge planner asked what had happened, the patient said, "I don't remember what I complained about, but whatever it was they took care of it, and they even sent me a pizza! I definitely want them back again!" The sales rep and I both just laughed. Patients don't remember when you correct mistakes, but they really remember if you wow them.

I also recommend that you study your staff's skills assessments. A skill assessment is a tool that each clinical staff member fills out when he or she is hired. On it, the staff member rates how well he or she would be able to complete each skill. By aggregating the results each year on each new hire, you will be able to identify what you need to plan for the following year's employee training and in-service. Growth needs to be supported by everyone at your organization. Unfortunately, all of us are only as good as our weakest employee. Studying the data above will help you identify that employee and prevent poor customer service experiences.

You also need to set new goals each year. Before doing so, perform another SWOT analysis and have the data above aggregated. Your goals should be based on areas that were addressed in your SWOT. Set realistic goals. Review your prior year's goals to see if you reached them. Share your goals, as well as the review of the previous year's goals, with your staff. Be honest when reviewing your goals. If you didn't accomplish a goal, find out why. Do you still want it as a goal for this year, or did something change so that the goal is no longer relevant? I remind you that your SWOT should be done with your management team as well as all of your sales representatives. Every time you do a SWOT, compare it with your previous one.

11

Replication and Conclusion

IN 2013, WHEN I WON SALES MANAGER OF the Year, agencies in the audience when I spoke about my steps to sales success contacted me to ask me to help them do the same thing. I took on several clients for free. I wanted to see if I could replicate the success. I was thrilled to see that my five steps to sales success worked over and over again. I also tried it with different sizes of agencies, private duty only, and hospice only providers. Again, I was able to replicate the success. At the end of 2013, I opened Penta Care Consulting.

In August 2013, I was invited to join Home Care Sales. I love working with Melanie. I love my job. You can replicate the success by following my 5 Steps to Success. If you need some help, please visit my website www.homecaresales.com or visit https://cherylpeltekis.enterprises.

I am available to speak at any conference or coorporate events. Presentations can be tailored to the audience's outcomes.

No matter what's motivating you to grow your organization, you have already done the hard work. You got your organization open and operating. Congratulations! Now you just need to set a plan in place. Follow the 5 Steps to Success, and as you climb each step, you are passing your competition a little bit more. You can do this!

Please feel free to connect with me on LinkedIn. If you want to know the sales process that I used, it is called *The 5 Steps to High Performance Selling*, and you can download the free book at www.homecaresales.com.

2023: Update!

It is now time to prepared for Valued Based Purchasing. You can find customer survice training on our website. I would suggest you add this training to your orientation program. Under valued based purchasing your agency will be reimbursed based on outcome scores and customer service scores. VBP (Value based purchasing), will now reward agencies that get patients healthier. It is critical to make sure that your clinical staff knows how to answer the oasis assessment.

Hospice folks also have change coming. Moving to an assessment form potentially called Hope. This standarized assessment will ultimately allow each hospice agency's care be compared.

Private duty has the challenge of more seniors that need care than the number of caregivers available. The organizations with exceptional leadership will win and retain their employees.

The future is bright for all post acute care providers. We will all need to utizlize technologies to streamline communication. Technology can help with improving patient outcomes and replace caregivers by providing virtual interaction. We need divergent thinking on how patients care is scheduled and how our employees work. Those who can evolve to meet the current working climate will be the heros of our seniors. There is no better time to be a post acute care provider! I know you are up to the challenge.

Bibliography

"What is FISH!?" FISH. Accessed May 2, 2022. https://www.fishphilosophy.com/what-is-fish/.

www.ingramcontent.com/pod-product-compliance
Lightning Source LLC
Chambersburg PA
CBHW031535210526
45464CB00003B/1016